The Lovers' Handbook

GLORIA HARGREAVES

The
Lovers'
Handbook

Handwriting
and
Personal
Relationships

PETER OWEN · LONDON & CHESTER SPRINGS

To Phillip and Danielle

PETER OWEN PUBLISHERS
73 Kenway Road London SW5 0RE

Peter Owen books are distributed in the USA
by Dufour Editions Inc. Chester Springs PA
19425-0449

First published in Great Britain 1990
© Gloria Hargreaves 1990

British Library Cataloguing in
Publication Data

Hargreaves, Gloria
  The lovers' handbook
  1. Graphology
  1. Title
  155-282

ISBN 0-7206-0791-4

Printed in Great Britain by
Billings of Worcester

CONTENTS

	INTRODUCTION	7
1	How Reliable Are You?	9
2	Are You an Extrovert or an Introvert?	12
3	How Emotional Are You?	16
4	How Much Energy Do You Have?	18
5	How Decisive Are You?	20
6	Do You Have a Jealous Nature?	24
7	Are You Clear-Thinking or Confused?	26
8	How Truthful Are You?	28
9	How Well Do You Communicate Your Feelings?	30
10	Are You Logical or Intuitive?	35
11	How Do You Act in Social Situations?	38
12	Are You Tactful?	40
13	How Good Do You Feel About Yourself?	42
14	Do You Distance Yourself from Others?	47
15	How Do You Overcome Day-to-Day Obstacles?	54
16	Do You Have a Sense of Humour?	57
17	Are You Sexually Compatible?	59
18	Signatures: Your Personal Thumb-Print	64

INTRODUCTION

One in three marriages in this country now ends in divorce and one in four adults lives alone, frequently not from choice. Why is it that our relationships so often turn out to be unsuccessful? Are our expectations too high? Do we give too little and ask too much? Are we unable to recognize and work through problem areas? Or have we chosen the wrong partner in the first place?

People can modify their behaviour and attitude, but fundamental character change is much more difficult. So it is unlikely that someone who is not compatible with you in the beginning will become so later. But relationships that worked well once can work well again, given understanding and some effort on both sides. In a good relationship we allow our partner to grow, develop and mature; in a bad one both partners are likely to feel trapped and stifled. While there is no such thing as a *perfect* relationship, most of us can make the one we have as good as possible if there is a mutual wish to do so. To achieve this it helps greatly to have some insight into our own character and needs as well as those of our partner.

Handwriting analysis can here be of enormous assistance. It can show us ourselves as we really are and pinpoint problem areas in our relationship that may have become even more tangled through repeated arguments. For example, you may be accusing your partner of being intolerant, selfish or over-sensitive without realizing that you have your fair share of the same traits. At the same time you may be missing many positive qualities in your partner or yourself that you have not been aware of, let alone valued.

This handbook shows you how to spot positive as well as negative traits in your own and your partner's handwriting and provides you with the information you need to work out detailed character portraits of you both. Nothing could be simpler than reading, and noting, the interpretations that apply to your individual scripts and checking them against the many original handwriting samples illustrating the movements that are characteristic of different traits. While this will almost certainly result in some unexpected discoveries, it should lead you to a greater understanding of each other and offer you a better basis on which to build a future.

AIDS is with us now and is likely to be around for a long time. Trying to find happiness with your existing partner makes sense. Also, children suffer greatly when a relationship breaks up, so it is well worth exploring every avenue before taking the drastic measures entailed by separation or divorce. And it is a fact that most of us carry our existing problems into the next relationship or, alternatively, find a whole new set awaiting us. So pick up a pen and paper – and if possible get your partner to do the same – to see how you can help yourselves now. *Handwriting does not lie.*

1

How Reliable Are You?

Reliability and emotional stability are indicated by the *baseline* – the invisible line at the base of the middle-zone letters. A straight, even line demands control and will-power and is a good indicator of emotional adjustment.

baseline

STRAIGHT

I am . twenty eight of age and have been up for the same company

Your mind controls your emotions. You are a reliable partner. A good trait.

WAVERING

To live in the woods, to roam the hills and valleys, to soar over the foam

Your morals are a bit flexible. You should not let others influence you so much.

VERY ERRATIC

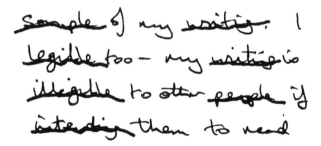

You are lacking in backbone and moral strength and are likely to be indecisive, unreliable and confused. You'll love them and leave them.

EXCESSIVELY RIGID

The time was near & she kn
hard bed of the Abbey guestho
stranger had stood in shadow.

You are over-controlled and frightened of letting others penetrate your thoughts. You can be explosive if control is lost.

WORDS RISING

difficult to write 'normally' w
are that someone will be

You are excitable, optimistic and easily aroused.

WORDS FALLING

is there any any
? Such, nowhere known some
li or braid or brace
ne catch or key to keep...

If done occasionally, indicates tiredness. If done repeatedly,
a sign of depression.

2

Are You an Extrovert or an Introvert?

The *size* of your writing shows how much value you place on yourself and how much you wish to impress others. The larger the writing, the more extroverted the personality. The very small writer will be more introverted and modest. Size should be measured from the top of the upper-case letter to the bottom of the lower-case letter.

The examples below show the three dominant sizes:

large size
9½ mm upwards

medium size   9 mm

small size 8½ mm or less

LARGE

*Very diplomatic and
ed   Smaller type face
ne   Portrayed thereabouts –
Sizeable different and
I can really go to.
?es , which flows with*

One thing is certain, life is never boring with these writers. Their greatest aim is to impress all around them. They seek recognition, and if you are not prepared to acknowledge in public how wonderful they are, you might as well give up now. They have great imagination and many leadership qualities. They enjoy working on large-scale projects, so don't ask them to replace the missing tile in the bathroom – they are much more likely to decide to redesign the whole of the ground floor. Minor details bore them, so it will help if you enjoy finishing off what they start! Their range of interests and activities is very wide – anything from amateur dramatics to golf – and you may have to resign yourself to playing second fiddle. Their optimism and enthusiasm never waver. They get enormous pleasure from buying extravagant gifts when the mood takes them. They are mainly cheerful partners. Sexually they have bags of imagination and generally the energy to convert it into practice. On the negative side, they can easily get bored and need a stimulating partner.

MEDIUM

I've always wanted to become a vet. I was just wandering what qualifications you needed.

Thanks

These writers are basically realistic and down-to-earth, and neither over- nor underestimate their own worth. They show a high degree of adaptability and, on the whole, make good partners who can adapt well to either the large or the small writer. They tend to buy totally appropriate gifts and enjoy a reasonable amount of entertaining. Their range of interests tends to harmonize with the amount of free time available. Sexually they are pretty undemanding but, with encouragement, very open to suggestion!

SMALL

Apologies for not writing sooner. After reading Sze's letter, dreams of going over to London were dashed. My disappointment was compounded? by the numerous unsuccessful interviews. Now, I'm very upset because my parent and relatives are against me working as a front office cashier. And because of this, I couldn't concentrate fully during work, hence now, I owe the hotel around $400 due to an oversight/carelessness on my part, letting the guest checked out without paying for the room charges and forgetting to imprint (blank) the Visit card account number on the charge form. The hotel has already written to the

These are the more introspective types who hate the limelight. Frequently shy, modest and retiring, they relate best to people they know well, so don't fill the house with strangers and expect a jolly time. Invite a few close friends and they will be at their happiest. Any jobs around the house that require close attention to detail will be welcomed. They don't part with their money lightly (unless it's for a special offer that promises them a saving). You are likely to receive occasional small, well-chosen gifts, but don't expect anything too extravagant. Many small writers have considerable executive ability but they are the thinkers, not the doers. Sex will not be madly exciting – more ritualistic, considered and caring.

3

How Emotional Are You?

Loops are known as the avenue of the emotions and they tell us a great deal about our responses.

Do you understand your partner's emotional needs? There can't be anything more crushing than to say, 'I love you' and be met by a deathly silence. Perhaps your partner would like to respond warmly but experiences great difficulty in doing so. Yet repressing our emotional needs can make us feel angry and frustrated, so it's important for both parties to understand what those needs are.

VERY WIDE

Great emotional need is shown here. Although a lot of problems can arise if both partners have excessive needs, it is essential to allow these needs to be expressed. This can be tiresome as, once encouraged, you could be opening the floodgates. But it is vital for emotionally needy people to have a listening ear, otherwise they might seek an alternative outlet!

AVERAGE

Evidence of emotional well-being. These writers get enough feedback in their relationship and feel happy and contented within it.

RETRACED OR NARROW

l l l

A lot of inhibition is shown here, indicating great difficulty in freely expressing feelings, even when encouraged. These are the types who will say, 'Didn't I tell you last year that I love you? Why do you want to hear it again?'

STRAIGHT STROKES

When the loop has been eliminated completely, we find sound judgement and a tendency for the head to rule the heart. These people do not have a great need to seek emotional support. They make very loyal partners and are often amazed when *their* partners complain that they are not receiving the emotional support *they* need.

MIXTURE OF STRAIGHT STROKES AND LOOPS

This is normally a good combination. Although these writers may have different reactions to the same situation on different occasions, they seem to have the understanding and intelligence to appreciate the other person's point of view. The mixture is often found in the handwriting of partners who have a satisfactory relationship.

In conclusion, when partners have very different loop formations, it is important to recognize these differences in order to understand the other person. Often this is half the battle towards accepting them.

4

How Much Energy Do You Have?

The degree of *pressure* you place on your pen shows how much energy you have available for your goals, pursuits and sex life. How do you rate?

Heavy

Medium

Light

Pasty

Feel the back of the paper with your thumb and index finger to test for pressure: strong indentation equals heavy pressure; slight indentation equals medium; no indentation equals light; pasty, which looks heavy, has no indentation. It is frequently produced by a felt tip or broad nib.

HEAVY

These are demanding types, both emotionally and physically. We always know when they are around. They are forceful and need to make an impression, easily excited and quick to respond. They can also be very stubborn and, on occasion, morose. If you want a fun time and a very active sex life, this is the partner for you – that is, if you have a high energy level yourself!

MEDIUM

The majority of us fall into this category, with sufficient energy to get by on a day-to-day basis. These writers show a healthy degree of vitality and will-power. Sexually they are neither over-ardent nor passive. On the whole, they make nice, considerate partners.

LIGHT

A lot of sensitivity is shown here, as well as some delicacy of feeling. These are very idealistic types who often feel disappointed with their fellow men. They are impressionable and can easily be dominated by a heavy-pressure writer. Their will-power is a little weak, energy levels are low, and there may be a tendency to think of sex as unclean. They are however quite good at role-playing, so dressing up has a certain appeal!

PASTY

These are very sensual types, warm natured and good humoured. They have a deep appreciation of new ideas and situations, see the whole world as colourful and are frequently artistic. They welcome tactile stimulation and are sexually very experimental. On the negative side, they do like change and variety. If your partner is one of these types, hang on to him or her! Playing helpless is a good idea here – they love the underdog.

5

How Decisive Are You?

The way you form your letters – from angular to rounded – reveals a lot about how decisions are taken in your relationship. There are five different *letter formations.*

ANGULAR

12 May 1986

s dismissed by the British sterday as being in the in some cases visions of its report rents ranging from n flower remedies were and negative by

You are highly intelligent, determined and mentally aggressive. You are also very good at sorting out major problems in your personal life, but run a mile when faced with minor difficulties or irritations. Human emotions tend to baffle you. You make a sexy, demanding, energetic partner.

GARLAND

"special" pen, and the great pleasure from the choices one has in - making.

You are passive, non-competitive and delightful, but you have difficulty in asserting yourself. Always willing to lend a helping hand, you could easily allow yourself to be treated like a doormat by a dominating personality. Home, family and friends mean a lot to you and you are very hospitable. As you have a strong need for security, you are responsive to a considerate partner but completely crushed by an aggressive one, as you hate conflict. You would experience great difficulty in sharing your life with an angular writer.

ARCADE

ssing is not the right career e. I leave my present n Hairdressing at the end of onth. I am now looking for a Career and wondered what ou tell me through my riting and my career decision

You express emotion in a very controlled way, do not welcome too much change and need the support of a reliable, caring partner. Socially you are a traditionalist but inwardly there lurks a bit of a rebel. You can be somewhat secretive, hiding a lot of your true feelings and thoughts. You take time to reach decisions but, once made, you stand by them firmly. Very loyal in relationships, you make a good, honest partner who gets along with most personalities.

THREAD-LIKE

after waiting

to think of

what one is going

to say. But when

You are somewhat unpredictable and can be difficult to pin down when decisions have to be made. You are very intuitive and love the arts. You are kind to your fellow men and look for appreciation rather than material gain, but you often feel unsure of yourself. High intelligence is shown, but you do not always know how to communicate it. As a partner you can be difficult, but you are always interesting. If the threading appears only at the end of a word, you are a born diplomat and negotiator.

Basically, I am forever changing my career plans. One day, I am adamant that teaching is the career for me, and the other,

Hard work does not appeal to you much. You find it difficult to get down to a job and have some lazy days. Decisions are put off until the last possible moment and you would much rather let others make them for you. Nevertheless, you have a lot of charm, you are kind to others and always willing to offer a helping hand – provided this does not call for too much energy!

6

Do You Have a Jealous Nature?

Jealousy is a most destructive trait. It can cause untold damage even in an otherwise good relationship. Here are some of the main indications:

Jealousy

'a' AND 'o' LARGER THAN OTHER LOWER-CASE LETTERS

A sure sign of someone who feels insecure with his or her partner and demands their full attention – otherwise outbursts might occur.

SMALL STARTING CIRCLE AT BEGINNING OF CAPITAL OR LOWER-CASE LETTER

Shows jealousy directed towards one particular individual.

LARGE STARTING CIRCLE AT BEGINNING OF CAPITAL OR LOWER-CASE LETTER

Shows jealousy towards a number of different people. Writers who produce this movement will complain about the amount of time given to their partner's employer, hobbies, etc.

LARGE STARTING CIRCLE ON BASE OF CAPITAL LETTER

Used by people who will put obstacles in your way to prevent you from giving time to anything other than their needs.

7

Are You Clear-Thinking or Confused?

Spacing between lines is a measure of mental clarity and orderliness.

ONE LINE TANGLING WITH THE NEXT

People who write like this are often lively and forceful but they have difficulty in ordering their thoughts. Their concentration is bad and they don't find it easy to plan or organize anything. Confusion reigns. If you are organized yourself, these types could drive you insane. They are often stingy.

GOOD, CLEAR SPACING

Id I go back to my original
/ should I make a complete
a fresh career? My name is
twenty two years of age.

These are orderly thinkers who have the ability to explain things to others. Their writing shows good powers of concentration, flexibility and personal harmony. They make good committee members. They also enjoy organizing the family.

VERY WIDE SPACING

Today in the nicest weekend

that I've experienced in

many a day.

Although clear-thinking, these people are not able to communicate their ideas. They are usually distrustful of other people's motives and find it difficult to relate socially. They can be extravagant on their own behalf and occasionally generous to others. Basically withdrawn and quite isolated, they often feel different from the rest of the world and construct grandiose ideas for themselves.

8

How Truthful Are You?

Do you always tell the truth, find it easy to tell a 'white lie', or readily resort to lying? *Ovals* like 'a' and 'o' tell us a lot about how truthful we are in general and how much of ourselves we reveal in our personal relationships.

CLOSED

You think before you speak, and you tell the truth. You are basically quite reserved in your speech.

OPEN TO RIGHT

You are quite talkative and speak the truth directly to the person concerned. You despise liars.

OPEN TO LEFT

You have a strong tendency to talk behind others' backs and have been known to embroider the truth.

OPEN WITH KNOTS

You utter the first words that come into your mind and they are often far from the truth.

LOOPED AND KNOTTED

Even when it would be easy for you to tell the truth, you tend to tell white lies.

KNOTTED ON LEFT

You take pleasure in lying and enjoy deceiving others.

KNOTTED ON RIGHT

Lying has become such a habit for you that you can't even remember what the truth really is.

NARROW AND KNOTTED

You are selective in what you tell your partner and often lie by omission.

FINAL STROKE TO LEFT

A very self-protective sign. It indicates that you always have a quick answer to hand and are able to 'bend' the truth.

OPEN AT TOP

You are talkative but honest and sincere.

BROAD AND CLOSED

You are broad-minded. You let others have their say and also make a good listener.

NARROW AND CLOSED

You are frightened to speak the truth and frequently remain silent.

9

How Well Do You Communicate Your Feelings?

Slant – the angle of writing in relation to the baseline – is an indication of the way we relate to the world and reveals a great deal about our ability to communicate thoughts, feelings and needs to others. Slant can be divided into the following categories:

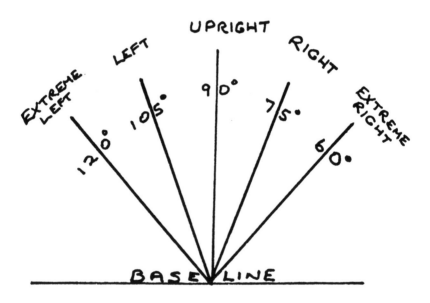

UPRIGHT

fully recovered show
of Trainee Chef, o
change and start
Denise and I'm
Please can

These are the most reliable of all types, with a head-ruling-the-heart emotional attitude. They can be difficult to catch but, being extremely loyal, rarely let you down once they are committed. They do not welcome great public displays of affection but a courtesy peck is quite acceptable. They enjoy sex with the one they love and suffer great pangs of guilt if they stray.

RIGHT

I am not for a moment
teaches or nurses for
Would do me same

These are emotionally healthy individuals with a fair degree of sensitivity, in the main sympathetic and compassionate. They can be reasonably demonstrative but won't encourage great outward displays of affection. Right slanters need a permanent partner as they have a lot of affection to give and like to plan for the future. They make good marriage partners. When it comes to lovemaking, they do like to take the initiative!

EXTREME RIGHT

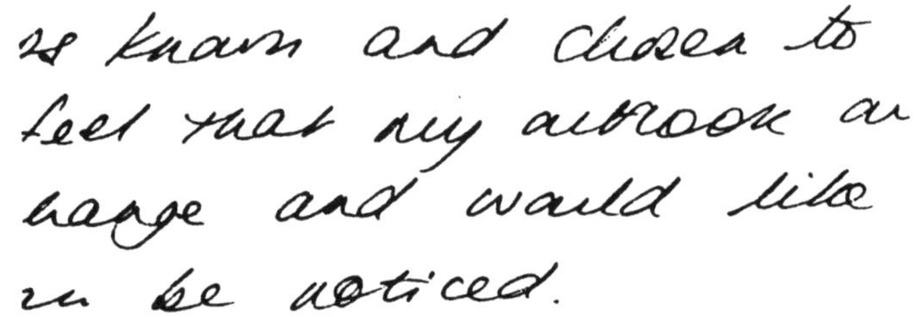

[handwritten text]

These are types who cry and laugh very easily. They love a weepy film and are suckers for hard-luck stories. They are quick to react – with either elation or dejection. Being in love is a constant trait of their personality, from the age of nine to well into the nineties. On the negative side, they cannot always decide where their true affection lies: it could be with you or with your best friend! They find it difficult to keep their hands off the opposite sex.

LEFT

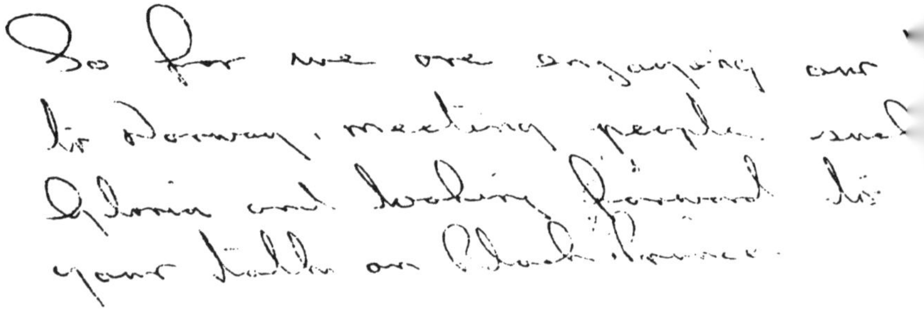

[handwritten text]

Caution is the name of the game here. On the surface these people are extremely charming, but they find it very difficult to commit themselves emotionally to anyone on a long-term basis. Once committed, though, they are yours for life. They tend to have rather unforgiving natures, so don't let them down! They also dislike last-minute changes of plan. Their mothers can be very important to them, so you could well find yourself part of a threesome. They also enjoy visiting museums, art galleries and old buildings, and talk a lot about the past. They can make very good lovers but may need some encouragement along the way.

EXTREME LEFT

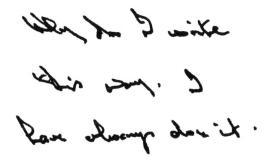

This is fairly uncommon, but if you do meet one of these writers you will notice at once how evasive he or she can be. People in this category have extreme difficulty in expressing their emotional needs or in understanding yours. They tend to marry late in life and never really form a close relationship. Being excessively sensitive, they are quick to take offence. Life is never easy with an extreme-left slanter. In bed, the partner will need to take most of the initiative.

ERRATIC

If you want to make yourself unhappy, marry one of these! They will love you today and leave you tomorrow. Often

33

they make interesting and amusing companions, but not on a long-term basis. Communicative one day and silent the next, you never know where you are with them. They have been known to leave you at the altar! Sexually they are frustrating types, rearing to go one minute and claiming exhaustion the next.

10

Are You Logical or Intuitive?

Do you connect every letter, find it difficult to connect any letters, or come somewhere between the two? The way we make *letter connections*, or fail to do so, is related to how logical or intuitive we are. If one partner relies mostly on logic and the other largely on intuition, this can create misunderstandings and problems. How do you rate in this area?

totally connected

totally disconnected

some disconnections

TOTALLY CONNECTED

not that I'm not confident but I know that if I don't have to do any work then I don't! I have the basic ability but have always hoped (and teachers have said) that there

These are logical, systematic thinkers who are stimulated by a mental challenge. They strongly dislike being interrupted in any task they have undertaken and will always wait until they have reached an appropriate stopping point.

Socially they can be inconsiderate and tactless. They enjoy solving other people's problems, especially when they have not been invited to do so. On the other hand, they are not too good at solving their own, because the closer they are to something the greater their difficulty in seeing it clearly. They are not particularly sympathetic people – unless you are suffering from an ailment they too have suffered from. Then they are likely to go on about it at great length.

Sexually they tend to think of what has happened in the past or what might happen in the future, so they completely miss what is going on now. Any appeal made to this kind of person must be based on logic. So keep your emotions under control!

TOTALLY DISCONNECTED

I am a 17 year old student wi

I am stuck between to ambitior

the opposite I would like to be

I was reading this article ai

Could tell me what type of cc

These are the intuitive types whose opinions spring from feeling rather than reasoning. Occasionally they come up with brilliant ideas, but they often need help putting them into practice. Their minds could be described as being of the grasshopper variety!

They have strong likes and dislikes, so not everybody you introduce them to will be warmly received. They can be moody and restless, and may appear vague.

On the positive side, they are very sympathetic and often play 'Agony Aunt' to others while retaining a strong sense of their own individuality. Sexually they are inclined to call the tune but, when in the mood, they are interesting and imaginative lovers.

SOME DISCONNECTIONS

Down in a day dark ditch sat

old cow munching a beanstalk.

Here we have the best of both worlds – a combination of logic and intuition. These people keep on a fairly even keel: they are not as compulsive as the totally connected writer, nor as restless and moody as the totally disconnected one. They handle their problems well and are sensitive to the needs and wishes of others. This makes them very good friends and lovers, with a healthy appreciation of their own and their partner's sexual needs.

11

How Do You Act in Social Situations?

Broadness or narrowness in your letter formation is an indication of how you behave in a social situation. Are you socially outgoing or shy and self-conscious?

BROADNESS

[handwriting sample]

Broad writers are expansive in social situations. They love mixed company and are quite happy to allow their partners to circulate freely and talk to whomever they please, never feeling neglected if they are not included. They have a great sense of adventure and enjoy travel, feeling excited from the moment they start packing. They love open spaces, new places, walking, rambling and other outdoor pursuits. They also like large rooms in which they can spread themselves. They talk easily and enjoy change and variety in their friends and colleagues. All this makes them good hosts who love spending money on clothes, food and wine – sometimes to the point of extravagance.

With no inhibitions in their personal relationships, these types are easy to be with. Their sense of adventure and fun, linked with a lively imagination, makes sex very attractive too. But remember not to tie them to your apron strings – they cannot survive that. Given just a little freedom, they make very good, interesting partners.

NARROWNESS

aimed for medicine when I i
and now wouldn't want that 'r
Then I considered forensic su
dismissed acter having complet
realized that I didn't want

The narrow writer tends to be timid, self-conscious and hypersensitive. Scared of making fools of themselves, such people feel anxious in social situations. They are more secure in fairly small spaces and in places they know well. Holidays tend to be predictable – the same place as last year! They like you to be by their side and may panic if left alone at a party or social gathering. Their insecurity and basic distrust of people can lead to embarrassing situations: in a group of people whom they don't know well, they may feel 'cornered' or 'got at'.

On the positive side, they are completely loyal to their partner, family and friends. They also have a highly developed sense of economy, collecting bits oi string, screws, nails, etc., in case these might come in useful one day. Make sure the right tools are always to hand as improvisation does not come easily to narrow writers. Sexually they exercise a lot of restraint.

12

Are You Tactful?

The *size of the letters at the ends of your words* will show how you rate with regard to this particular trait.

DECREASING

A great deal of tact and diplomacy is shown here. You can safely introduce this writer to all your friends and family. He or she will also make you feel good about yourself by saying the right thing at the right moment. Nice to have around.

INCREASING

Think carefully before taking this writer home to meet your mother. He or she is likely to blurt out the first thought that comes to mind and could cause offence. Have you ever been told, 'That outfit would look great if you lost some weight'? This is the type of person who would think nothing of saying it!

SOME OF EACH

I have just written article in Over 21 magazine would be interested in... from my handwriting. I... handwriting and found.

Unpredictability is a problem. You can never be sure whether this writer will strike exactly the right note or cause you embarrassment. Interesting, but needs to be watched.

13

How Good Do You Feel About Yourself?

The *personal pronoun* 'I' shows how you feel about yourself and how you see yourself in relation to others.

19

SMALLER THAN REST OF SCRIPT
You don't value yourself enough.

I I

LARGER THAN REST OF SCRIPT
'Aren't I wonderful!' is the message you are shouting out to the world.

9 I

SAME SIZE AS SCRIPT
No pretence here. You are the same in public as in private.

2

LIKE THE FIGURE 2
Sadly, you feel second-rate. Frequently produced by people who have a clever brother or sister.

I

SINGLE PLAIN STROKE
You are genuine and see yourself as you are.

I

PRINTED
You think clearly and have a high opinion of yourself.

ı

LIKE A SMALL 'i'
You feel totally crushed and put down.

4

LIKE THE FIGURE 4
You cannot see anyone else's point of view.

g

AVERAGE-SIZE UPPER LOOP
You have a healthy self-respect.

ʃ

NARROW UPPER LOOP
You are timid and well aware of it.

g

WIDE UPPER LOOP
You are over-emotional and have an exaggerated sense of your own importance.

⌐

ARC TO LEFT
Irresponsibility is shown here. Try sticking to your commitments.

ᎦᏴ

HOOK TO LEFT
You can be greedy and unwilling to share.

TRIANGULAR BASE
Aggression can quickly surface.

CROSSED
Reveals strong fears and despondency.

DISCONNECTED STROKES
You are independent and love sporting activity.

SMALL WITH ADDITIONAL STROKES
You are uncertain of your own identity.

ANGULAR
You can be critical of yourself and hostile to others.

LARGE WITH ADDITIONAL FLOURISHES
A sign of vanity and vulgarity.

CURLED AND CLOSED
You have a self-protective and ungiving streak.

OPEN CIRCLE
You are looking for a mother figure.

LIKE A POUND SIGN
You see money as a source of personal value.

14

Do You Distance Yourself from Others?

—SPACING BETWEEN WORDS—

The space we leave between words shows the distance we like to maintain between ourselves and others.

VERY NARROW

People like this crave attention and can be quite selfish and insensitive to the needs of others. They are the types who butt in when you are having a private conversation with someone. If combined with very large handwriting, narrow spacing indicates generosity and even extravagance.

REGULAR, EVEN

I fully realise that no job is perfect, but I still feel that somewhere there is a job that really suit me; that I can get excited about. The aspect of my present job that I like most is meeting the new clients

These are discriminating types. They afford others the privacy they need but, if invited to join in, will do so with a good grace and will behave in a pleasant manner. They show intelligence and inner organization.

VERY WIDE

I do admit to being moody
, get quite down and
at times and seem to

These writers need to maintain some distance and can experience difficulty in communicating. They feel very isolated at times.

FILLING IN ALL SPACE

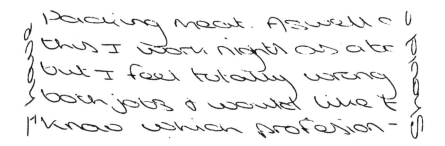

We all know people who write all around a card or letter, filling in every available bit of space. They are the ones who don't know when to stop talking or how to adapt their behaviour to suit the occasion. They say good-night half a dozen times on the doorstep and wake up all your neighbours at two o'clock in the morning, hooting their horn for good measure as they drive off. If you invite them, make sure you keep the whole day free!

MARGINS

Margins indicate the amount of space we need for ourselves.

BALANCED ALL ROUND

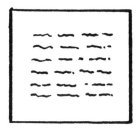

You don't put a foot wrong and treat all your family and friends with consideration and respect. You are a social asset, and also show good judgement.

WIDE ALL ROUND

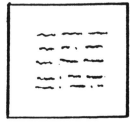

You can be aloof and uncertain about how to behave in social situations. You don't enjoy mixing and find it especially hard when you don't know people well.

WIDE LEFT

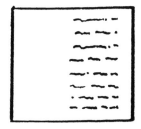

You are not too happy about the past but look to the future with a more positive attitude. Formality appeals to you; although you try hard to communicate well with others it does not come naturally.

WIDE RIGHT

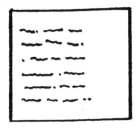

You are preoccupied with yourself at this moment and are wondering what the future holds in store for you. You find it difficult to face reality and are a poor mixer.

NARROWING LEFT

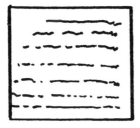

You are in the habit of making promises you know you can't fulfil. You also experience difficulty in moving forward and making decisions.

WIDENING LEFT

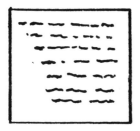

You are impatient, enthusiastic and expressive, and you find it hard to save money. You can become very absorbed in your interests and hobbies.

DEEP TOP

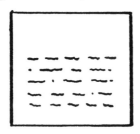

You like formality and show a great deal of respect for other people. You are also a caring person and you take the emotional and sexual needs of your partner into consideration.

SHALLOW TOP

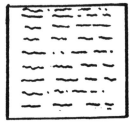

Your needs always have to come first. You show a lack of consideration for others, with a tendency towards tactless and clumsy behaviour.

DEEP LOWER

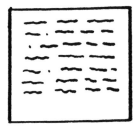

Your interest in other people quickly dissipates and you avoid commitment. You can be over-sensitive and take offence too quickly.

SHALLOW LOWER

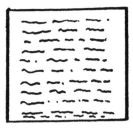

You have a tendency to become depressed. On some days you are completely uncommunicative, on others you are overbearing and no one else can get a word in. You lack self-discipline and are inclined to waste your energies.

NO MARGINS

Anything goes when you are around – you rush in where angels fear to tread. Who says everyone finds you interesting? You can go right over the top, and you love spending money – but only on yourself!

UNEVEN

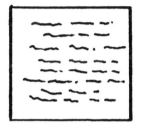

You are impulsive and a rebel, with a dislike of sensible rules and regulations. You invite strong positive and negative reactions from other people. Think before you speak! Rudeness comes easily to you.

15

How Do You Overcome Day-to-Day Obstacles?

The strength of your will-power and drive when coping with everyday challenges is shown by your *'t' crossings.*

SMALL
Shows timidity. You can't easily overcome problems as your will-power is weak.

BALANCED AND FIRM
You know what you want and use perfectly reasonable means to attain your goals.

LARGE
You go to any lengths to get what you want. Be careful you don't step on others in the process!

ABOVE DOWNSTROKE
You are quite unrealistic. Come down to earth!

TO THE RIGHT OF DOWNSTROKE
Slow down! You are in too much of a hurry and could overlook important details.

TO THE LEFT OF DOWNSTROKE
Your motto is, 'Don't do anything today that you can do tomorrow.'

NO CROSSING
By the time you get down to anything, you have forgotten what you wanted to do in the first place.

DOUBLE CROSSING
You show lack of confidence. You slow yourself down by checking and re-checking everything you do.

STRAIGHT AND RESTING ON TOP
You have high ideals and a strong will. You are also very protective towards family and friends.

VERY LOW
You feel inferior and always bow to the wishes of others.

ANGULAR
You are stubborn and determined, and you hate taking advice from anyone.

WAVY
You achieve a lot of what you set out to do, with the help of your lovely sense of humour.

CONCAVE
You are self-indulgent and tend to forget about the needs of others.

CONVEX
Shows discipline. You exercise a lot of control over your needs and drive.

CIRCULAR KNOT
You are a positive person and an achiever, but you act in a pleasant manner.

LOOPED STEM
You are quite vain and you try to attain your goals by using your charm.

FALLING
You give up easily and don't achieve a lot.

RISING
You are enthusiastic and try hard to achieve.

Note
Most of us will produce, say, two different crossings in the same piece of script, which is quite acceptable. Both interpretations will be valid. But a large variety of crossings does indicate some confusion between thoughts and actions.

16

Do You Have a Sense of Humour?

Seeing the funny side of life and not taking yourself too seriously can be of great help in overcoming difficulties together. Often when emotions reach boiling point, one or both partners will say or do something ridiculous that can change a tense atmosphere to one of laughter. But not everyone is secure enough to take such a self-detached view of themselves. When trying to spot a sense of humour in yourself or your partner, look for any stroke – or any letter of the alphabet – written in three directions (*three-way stroke*). These are some of the most common forms:

Shows a sense of fun and a talent for mimicry.

These writers laugh easily and look for the funny side of things.

These are our practical jokers.

Here we see our vulgar jokers – types who love telling dirty stories in the pub!

17

Are You Sexually Compatible?

The way we form the *loop on a 'g' or 'y'* is a good indication of our response in this important area of a relationship.

g

THE 'PERFECT LOVE LETTER'
A loving, warm person who is able to find contentment with one partner.

g *y*

ARCADED TO LEFT
Doesn't welcome responsibility in this area. If male, could run if you got pregnant.

g *y*

VERY NARROW LOOP
Finds difficulty in expressing sexual needs.

g *y*

VERY SHORT LOOP OR DOWNSTROKE
Little interest in sex, mainly because of lack of energy.

_9 y_

SWINGING LEFTWARD MOVEMENT
A constant need for change and variety. Will try many different partners but is unlikely to be content with any one.

_9 y_

STRAIGHT LEFTWARD STROKE
Enjoys self-gratification (masturbation).

_9 y_

CURLY DOWNSTROKE
An interesting partner. You need to be a bit of an athlete here – the missionary position will not satisfy this adventurous character.

_g y_

VERY LOW ROUNDED LOOP
Hasn't yet found sexual satisfaction – an insensitive partner, perhaps?

_g_

DOWNSTROKE WITH HEAVY PRESSURE, UPSTROKE WITH LIGHT PRESSURE
May start energetically but soon falls asleep at your side. If male, the type who boasts about the good time he can give you in bed.

DOWNSTROKE WITH LIGHT PRESSURE, UPSTROKE WITH HEAVY PRESSURE

They take a long time to get going but will surprise you with their agility and sexual adventurousness.

HOURGLASS FORMATION ON LOWER LOOP

People who handle other people's bodies – nurses, doctors, etc. – produce this particular movement. Suggests a clinical approach.

EXAGGERATED AND UNUSUAL MOVEMENTS

Often found in the handwriting of individuals with lesbian or homosexual tendencies, either active or latent.

BREAK IN UPSTROKE

Most commonly found in men who have had a vasectomy or women with gynaecological problems.

HOOKED ENDING ON UPSTROKE

These people are so concerned about their own enjoyment that they forget you are participating.

SMALL ANGLE
Tyrannical nature due to sexual frustration.

LARGE ANGLE
Really aggressive due to sexual frustration.

REVERSED ENDING
Sublimates sexual urges by doing good works.

HEAVY PRESSURE WITH INFLATED LOWER LOOP
Strong sexual appetite. Three times a day, and isn't going to let up!

STRAIGHT DOWNSTROKE
Will instigate sex only when they feel like it. A selfish partner.

g y

UPSTROKE STOPS SHORT
Enjoys the chase and the flirting but fears penetration.

g y

ANGLED AND LOOPED DOWNSTROKE
The type who always leaves the light on and loves to look at their own and their partner's naked body. Sexually vain.

g y

TICK ON DOWNSTROKE
A very nervous partner who needs a lot of encouragement and reassurance.

Note
A writer who always produces his or her 'g' and 'y' in the same way shows little imagination in the sexual act. Half a dozen different types of loop show someone who is easily turned on and has some lack of control. The average person produces two to three different loop (or straight-stroke) formations, indicating a healthy, imaginative interest in sex.

18

Signatures: Your Personal Thumb-Print

Your *signature* shows how you would like other people to see you.

Same Size

Anne Jones

LEGIBLE, SAME SIZE AS SCRIPT
You behave the same in public as in private. A genuine person.

Please do this as quickly as possible.

Elaine D'Angelo

LARGE IN RELATION TO REST OF SCRIPT
You seek recognition and could be hiding a feeling of inferiority.

FIRM UNDERLINE
You have a good degree of confidence.

DOUBLE UNDERLINE
You are putting yourself above others.

SMALL IN RELATION TO REST OF SCRIPT
You make a pretence of modesty.

SMALL UNDERLINE AT END
You would like to have the last word but doubt whether
you'll get away with it.

LINE ABOVE AND BELOW
You are self-protective and do not trust others.

LINE THROUGH LOWER-CASE LETTERS
Your self-esteem is low and you have a poor self-image.

ENCLOSED IN A CIRCLE
You try to hide your true intentions.

'T' CROSSING EXTENDED OVER REST OF LETTERS
You are very protective towards family and friends.

RISING
You are professionally ambitious.

FALLING
You may have been depressed or tired at the time of writing.

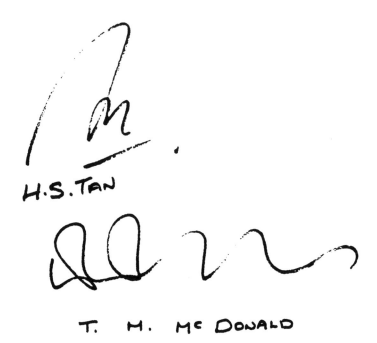

H.S. TAN

T. M. Mc DONALD

ILLEGIBLE
You are secretive and lack consideration. However, if you are in the habit of signing a lot of letters every day, it could merely suggest that you have a quick mind.

FULL STOP AFTER
You always want the last word.

TWO FULL STOPS AFTER
You always insist that you are right.

WAVY UNDERLINE
You have a nice sense of humour and you don't take yourself too seriously.

UNNECESSARY ADDITION TO FIRST STROKE
You have a habit of putting obstacles in other people's way.

UNNECESSARY ADDITION TO LAST STROKE
You don't know when to stop talking about yourself.

VERY ELABORATE UNDERLINING
You tend to be over-familiar – someone who immediately gets on to first-name terms.

J.M. Sprake

USE OF INITIALS ONLY
You are cautious – or formal in appropriate circumstances.

Catriona Marshall.

USE OF FULL NAME
You are a friendly person who likes to put others at their ease.

CHRISTIAN NAME AND SURNAME JOINED
You aim to make the maximum use of your personality.

SURNAME LARGER
You have a lot of respect for your husband or father.

David Smallwood

SURNAME SMALLER
If you are a woman, you appear to be unhappy with your partner; if a man, you don't feel much respect for your father.

Simon T. Bates

SMALL MIDDLE INITIAL
You dislike that particular name.

The following pages are left blank

for you to note the sections that apply

to your particular handwriting

(Your friends may also be included if you wish)

FOR YOUR OWN USE

FOR YOUR OWN USE

FOR YOUR OWN USE

FOR YOUR OWN USE

FOR YOUR OWN USE

FOR YOUR OWN USE

FOR YOUR OWN USE